OUR FUTURE IN SPACE

SPACE EXPLORERS
FROM EARTH TO INFINITY

David Jefferis

Crabtree Publishing Company
www.crabtreebooks.com

INTRODUCTION

Exploration beyond our world began in 1957, when the world's first **artificial satellite**, Sputnik 1, was fired into space. The Russian Yuri Gagarin became the first human in space in 1961, and just eight years after that, US astronauts Neil Armstrong and Buzz Aldrin set foot on the Moon.

But the Moon is as far as humans have ventured so far. All missions farther than the Moon have been carried out by uncrewed space probes. Will humans join machines to explore deep space in the future? Read on to find out!

↑ Sputnik 1 was a 23-inch (58 cm) metal sphere. Long radio antennas beamed signals back to Earth.

🌲 **Crabtree Publishing Company**
www.crabtreebooks.com   1-800-387-7650

Written and produced for Crabtree Publishing by:
David Jefferis

Technical advisor:
Mat Irvine FBIS (Fellow of the British Interplanetary Society)

Editors:
Mat Irvine, Janine Deschenes

Prepress Technicians:
Mat Irvine, Ken Wright

Proofreader:
Petrice Custance

Print Coordinator:
Margaret Amy Salter

Acknowledgements
We wish to thank all those people who have helped to create this publication and provided images.
Individuals:
    David Jefferis
    Gavin Page
    Luca Oleastri/Fotolia
    Mark Rademaker
Organisations:
    Aerospatiale
    Airbus Defence and Space
    Alcatel Alenia Space
    Arianespace
    Ball Aerospace
    Blue Origin
    Boeing Corp
    Canadian Space Agency
China News
ESA European Space Agency
Google
John Hopkins Applied Physics
    Laboratory
JPL Jet Propulsion Laboratory
Lockheed Martin
Microsatellite Systems
    Canada Inc
Mondoworks
NASA Space Agency
NASDA, JAXA, Japanese
    Space Agencies
Northrop Grumman
SETI Institute
SpaceX
United Launch Alliance
US Air Force

The right of David Jefferis to be identified as the Author of this work has been asserted by him in accordance with the Copyrights, Designs and Patents Act 1988.

Printed in the USA/102017/CG20170907

Library and Archives Canada Cataloguing in Publication

Jefferis, David, author
        Space explorers / David Jefferis.

(Our future in space)
Includes index.
Issued in print and electronic formats.
ISBN 978-0-7787-3535-9 (hardcover).--
ISBN 978-0-7787-3540-3 (softcover).--
ISBN 978-1-4271-1941-4 (HTML)

        1. Outer space--Exploration--Juvenile literature. 2. Space flight--Juvenile literature. I. Title.

TL793.J445 2017   j629.4   C2017-905186-5
                                                          C2017-905187-3

Library of Congress Cataloging-in-Publication Data

Names: Jefferis, David, author.
Title: Space explorers / David Jefferis.
Description: New York, New York : Crabtree Publishing Company, [2018]
    I Series: Our future in space I Includes index.
Identifiers: LCCN 2017044204 (print) I LCCN 2017045391 (ebook) I
    ISBN 9781427119414 (Electronic HTML) I
    ISBN 9780778735359 (reinforced library binding : alk. paper) I
    ISBN 9780778735403 (pbk. : alk. paper)
Subjects: LCSH: Outer space--Exploration--History--Juvenile literature. I
    Astronautics--United States--History--Juvenile literature.
Classification: LCC TL793 (ebook) I LCC TL793 .J435 2018 (print) I
    DDC 919.9/204--dc23
LC record available at https://lccn.loc.gov/2017044204

CONTENTS

4   Our Place in Space

6   Biggest Rockets ever Built

8   New Flags on the Moon

10   Eyes in the Sky

12   Exploring Deep Space

14   Return to the Furnace World

16   Rovers on the Red Planet

18   Exploring the Icy moons of Jupiter

20   Life on Saturn's moons?

22   Voyage into Darkness

24   Planets of Other Stars

26   Starshot to Alpha Centauri

28   Spaceships of the Far Future

30   Glossary

31   Websites and Further Information

32   Index and About the Author

OUR PLACE IN SPACE

We live on planet Earth, one of the planets that circle, or **orbit**, a star we call the Sun. This whole group is called the Solar System.

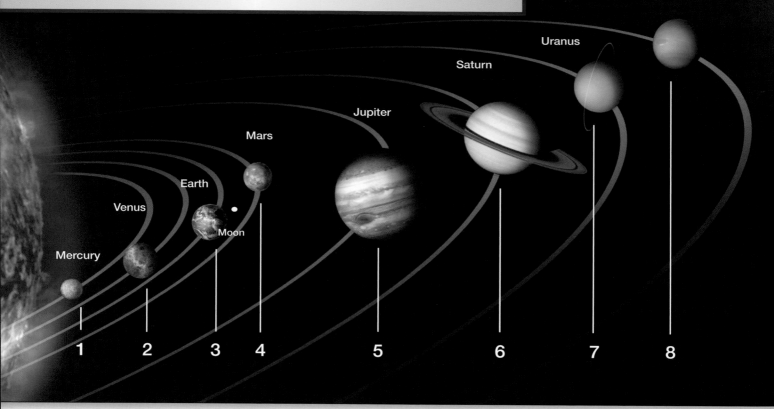

Neptune

Uranus

Saturn

Jupiter

Mars

Earth

Venus

Moon

Mercury

1 2 3 4 5 6 7 8

→ How many planets are there?
Our **Solar System** has eight major planets, including Earth. It also has smaller, dwarf planets, such as distant Pluto. All of these planets, except Mercury and Venus, have smaller objects orbiting them. These include natural satellites, or moons.

↑ The eight major planets, shown here numbered outward from the Sun:
1 Mercury, 2 Venus, 3 Earth, 4 Mars, 5 Jupiter, 6 Saturn, 7 Uranus, 8 Neptune.

→ How many planets have we explored?
Humans have been as far as Earth's Moon, but no farther. However, **robotic** spacecraft have been to every major planet, and flown closely past Pluto. Other targets for exploration include **comets** and **asteroids**. Countless numbers of these chunks of ice and rock are left over from the birth of our Solar System.

➔ Where do humans fly in space?

Since the **Apollo** Moon landings of 1969-72, humans have gone only as far as low Earth orbit (LEO). This is where the International Space Station (**ISS**) circles our planet, at about 250 miles (400 km) above Earth.

➔ Where will we go next?

A return to the Moon is a likely next step, though probably not before the mid-2020s. Beyond the Moon, the planet Mars is the most Earthlike world in the Solar System. A Mars mission carrying a human crew is a long-term aim for a number of space agencies. Mars is also a prime target for SpaceX, a California-based rocket company.

↑ The ISS is a multi-national base and science laboratory that orbits Earth. It will be in use until at least the mid-2020s.

➔ Where will future robotic missions go?

There are plenty of exploration missions being planned. These range from probing the Moon and Mars, to exploring the icy moons of Jupiter. The New Horizons space probe has already flown past the dwarf planet Pluto, beyond Neptune. Right now, and for many years to come, New Horizons will continue to explore the lonely regions of space that lie even farther away.

↑ In the near future, we could build a permanent Moon base. Much of the work will be done by robots. Humans would go to live there when the base is ready.

BIGGEST ROCKETS EVER BUILT

The Saturn V rocket, used for Moon flights, has long been the largest space launcher of all. But new designs could be even bigger.

Flight deck of the Dragon V2

→ What new rockets are being planned?

Several designs may replace the rockets of yesterday and the retired Space Shuttle. These include **NASA's** Space Launch System (SLS). Powerful enough to send vehicles far into the Solar System, the SLS could become the United States' main rocket. Private companies SpaceX and Blue Origin also have competing designs. SpaceX's Falcon rocket will carry the Dragon V2 spacecraft into space to transport crew to the ISS. SpaceX is also working on an Interplanetary Transport System (ITS) that could carry 100 people at a time.

↓ Size comparison:
1 Space Shuttle, 2 Soyuz, 3 Falcon 9,
4 Falcon Heavy, 5 New Glenn,
6 SLS, 7 Saturn V, 8 ITS.

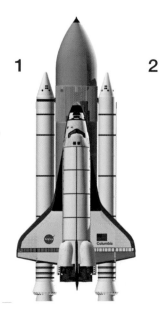

↑ Boeing is developing the 7-seat Starliner spacecraft to transport crews. It looks similar to the 3-seat Apollo capsule used for Moon flights from 1969-72.

→ Will new technology make space travel safer?

Two of NASA's five Space Shuttles were destroyed in accidents. All astronauts on board were killed. New safety measures and technologies arise after an accident, but spaceflight is still a risk.

→ What new spacecraft are being developed?

After the final Space Shuttle mission in 2011, the only way to reach the ISS was to fly in a Russian **Soyuz** spacecraft. Developing new spacecraft for humans, such as the Starliner and Dragon V2, and launchers powerful enough to lift them into orbit, has taken several years.

SPACE ROCK MISSION

A future mission could include visiting an asteroid, which is a chunk of rock orbiting the Sun. The crew would gather information about the rock's makeup as it traveled near Earth and the Moon.

NEW FLAGS ON THE MOON

Another Moon landing by humans is still years away. But the Moon is a prime destination for all kinds of scientific research missions.

Eugene Cernan was the last human on the Moon, in 1972

→ Who wants to go to the Moon, and why?

Reaching the Moon is a boost for any country's science and technology. It also gives them international recognition. The United States, Russia, Canada, and Europe are familiar to us as space explorers. Now, China, India, and Japan, as well as private companies, are also trying to reach the Moon.

↑ **The Chinese Moon rover Chang'e-3 landed in 2013. Future plans include collecting samples of Moon dust for return to Earth.**

→ What is the Google Lunar XPRIZE?

The Internet company Google funds the Lunar XPRIZE competition, with a top prize of $20 million. Earning that prize is not easy. The winner has to land a rover safely on the Moon and travel at least 1640 feet (500 m). It also has to send pictures and videos back to Earth as proof.

↑ The Orion spacecraft could take a crew of seven around the Moon.

→ Are any flights planned with human crews?

The US Space Launch System (SLS) will fly astronauts near the Moon, though not down to the surface. SpaceX plans to fly near-Moon flights with its Dragon V2 capsule, and eventually aims to land on Mars.

→ Will humans land on the Moon again?

At present, there is no such mission ready to fly. But several countries, including China and India, aim to land their astronauts there by the late 2020s, or perhaps before.

→ When can I go to the Moon?

Your best plan is to wait for SpaceX, or its rival Blue Origin, to start ticket sales. SpaceX already flies to the ISS with its Dragon capsule, and this could be modified to make landings on the Moon or Mars.

DID APOLLO HAPPEN?

Collins

Aldrin

Armstrong

Claims that the Apollo landings from 1969-72 were hoaxes don't hold up. Photos of the Moon taken since confirm it. The base section of the Lunar Module used by Armstrong and Aldrin is clearly visible.

EYES IN THE SKY

Space telescopes are astronomers' eyes in deep space. The James Webb Space Telescope (JWST) will be larger and provide more detail than previous designs, including the Hubble Space Telescope.

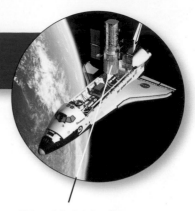

The Hubble Space Telescope was launched in 1990

→ **How many space telescopes are there?**

More than 30 **space telescopes** have been launched since the 1980s. The best known is the Hubble Space Telescope (HST), which was launched in 1990 to orbit Earth.

Astronauts from the Space Shuttle *Atlantis* performed maintenance on the HST in 2009. Since then, the space telescope has performed well. No further maintenance has been planned since Space Shuttle flights ended in 2011.

↑ **The JWST main mirror is made up of 18 gold-coated, six-sided segments. The segments are easier and cheaper to make than one larger mirror. Once the telescope reaches space, the segments will be unfolded.**

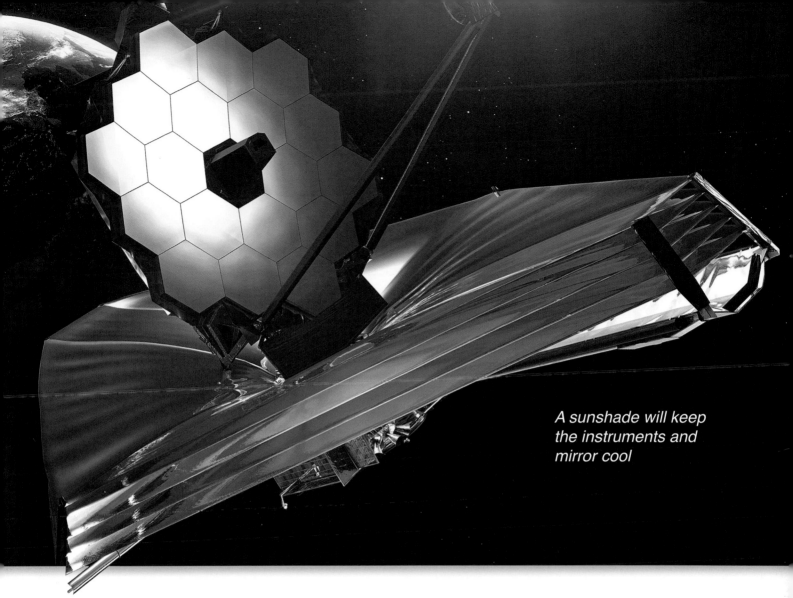

A sunshade will keep the instruments and mirror cool

↑ The JWST is an infrared telescope. This means it "sees" by sensing radiation invisible to the human eye.

➜ Where did the JWST get its name?

The JWST is named after James Webb, the man who was in charge of NASA, from 1961-68. His main focus then was the NASA Apollo program, which aimed to land humans on the Moon.

➜ When will the JWST be launched?

The JWST will take off in 2018, using an Ariane 5 rocket to place it on orbit approximately 930,000 miles (1.5 million km) from Earth. The JWST is an international project between NASA and other countries, including the space agencies of Canada and Europe.

CANADA'S MOST TELESCOPE

Canada's first space telescope was launched in 2003. The size of a suitcase, MOST (Microvariability and Oscillation of Stars) records the surface movements of stars. It also confirmed the existence of a new planet orbiting another star.

EXPLORING DEEP SPACE

Three robotic space probes will travel far beyond Earth, with the aim of discovering secrets of the Solar System's distant past.

→ Where are the probes going?

The targets are various asteroids, all space rocks left over from the creation of the Solar System. Scientists are interested because such asteroids have remained almost unchanged for billions of years. Studying them helps us piece together the ancient story of how the planets formed.

NASA's three asteroid probes are called Lucy, OSIRIS-REx, and Psyche.

↑ In 2025, Lucy will arrive at the first of six asteroids called Trojans, in a similar orbit to the planet Jupiter. Lucy will go from asteroid to asteroid, studying them over an eight-year period.

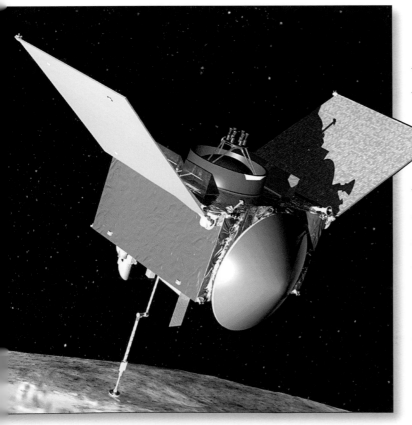

→ What will OSIRIS-REx do?

It has a seven-year mission, during which the probe will approach the asteroid Bennu, then descend to the surface at less than walking pace. A robotic arm's landing pad will touch Bennu and take a small sample of dust. The arm will then pack the sample safely into a cone-shaped capsule for travel back to Earth. In 2023, the sample will be parachuted down to land safely in Utah in the United States.

← OSIRIS-REx will study Bennu because it could become dangerous in the future. It is an "impactor" asteroid, which means it might hit Earth. A collision could take place in the 22nd century, resulting in massive damage.

→ What is Psyche?

The Psyche probe is named after its target asteroid— 16 Psyche. The asteroid is unusual because it is made mostly of iron and nickel, rather than rock or stone.

It is thought that 16 Psyche could be the remains of a planet that was once the size of Mars. Eight years after launch in 2022, the space probe may confirm that 16 Psyche is a part of the core of that ancient planet, blown apart in a series of huge, cosmic collisions.

↑ Pysche will explore the only known metallic asteroid.

→ Space collisions were common in the early years of the Solar System's formation.

HOW ARE SPACE PROBES NAMED?

Spacecraft are usually given interesting names. These three probes are no exception:

OSIRIS-REx is short for Origins, Spectral Interpretation, Resources Identification, Security, and Regolith Explorer. Osiris was the ancient Egyptian god of the dead.

Lucy was named after the fossil skeleton of a pre-human ape. Psyche is named after its target asteroid.

RETURN TO THE FURNACE WORLD

Space probes have shown that the surface of the planet Venus roasts at a temperature of about 880°F (470°C). Now there are plans to send more probes there.

The Russian Venera 10 landed on Venus in 1975

→ **Is heat the only problem with a Venus expedition?**
The atmosphere on Venus would also be unbreathable. It is mainly carbon dioxide gas. The surrounding gases are so thick, the **pressure** is up to 93 times greater than on Earth. Russia has sent several Venera landers to Venus. The longest survivor was crushed by the pressure of the atmosphere in less than two hours.

Conditions on Venus may have been similar to Earth once. When Venus lost its water, the environment became deadly.

↑ The eight-legged machine above is a possible design for a future Venus **rover**. Power comes from a **wind turbine,** which would use the high winds of Venus to charge onboard batteries.

➜ Could a probe operate anywhere on Venus?

The surface of Venus is deadly, but conditions in the upper atmosphere are far less extreme. In fact, the US scientist Geoffrey Landis believes that 30 miles (50 km) up, the temperature and atmospheric pressure are the most similar to Earth of all the Solar System's planets.

An airship-laboratory could safely float at that height. Researchers on board could carry out long-term studies.

⬆ It might be possible for an airship laboratory to float safely, high above the acid clouds of Venus. This illustration imagines a group of larger balloons connected together to form a base or sky city.

WHAT CAN VENUS TEACH US?

Venus is important for studying the effects of a lot of carbon dioxide gas in the atmosphere. Carbon dioxide helps trap heat inside Earth's atmosphere causing the planet's temperature to rise. Global warming is a big concern of climate experts. Will increased carbon dioxide emissions lead to Earth overheating like Venus?

Earth

Venus

➜ How long could I survive on the surface?

Without a protective suit, you would die almost instantly. In a second or two, you would be boiled by the heat, and crushed by pressure from the surrounding gases. If you somehow survived a little longer, you would breathe in the deadly sulfuric acid contained in the clouds.

ROVERS ON THE RED PLANET

 Roving vehicles have been exploring Mars—the red planet—since 1997. New rovers will be sent there in years to come.

Sojourner was the first Mars rover. It landed in 1997.

↑ NASA's Curiosity rover landed on Mars in 2012. Still on Mars today, it continues to study its geology and climate. The rover has also been looking for signs of Martian life.

→ **What have exploration rovers found on Mars?**

Mars rovers and orbiting satellites have revealed a fascinating world. Mars has Olympus Mons, the highest volcano in the Solar System. The canyon Valles Marineris is far bigger than the Grand Canyon on Earth. Shallow seas once covered much of Mars. The seas are gone, but many scientists think evidence of water may mean there was once life on the planet. Perhaps some simple forms survive today.

Mastcam to take
pictures and videos

Equipment to
test whether
oxygen can be
produced from
the atmosphere

Metal wheels
with special
treads to climb
steep slopes

Ground-penetrating
radar to map what is
below the surface

→ When will another rover go to Mars?
The next Mars rover is targeted to touch down in 2020. Its design is based on the Curiosity rover, and a main aim is to search for signs of Martian life, past or present.

The rover will also collect soil and rock samples to be sent back to Earth by a later mission.

↑ The Mars 2020 rover is a **six-wheel design. Its instruments include microphones to record the sounds of Mars.**

→ What about human explorers?
Flights to Mars are long and dangerous. To date, nearly half of all robotic missions have failed to arrive. Even so, both NASA and SpaceX are aiming to send crewed flights in the future.

BRINGING HOME A PIECE OF RED PLANET
The next step for Mars exploration will be to bring samples back to Earth. Rocks will be loaded aboard a small rocket (left) which will be sent back to Earth.
Being able to examine rocks firsthand will maybe help researchers understand the red planet's geology.

The giant planet Jupiter and its many moons have been studied by space probes since the 1970s.

NASA's Pioneer 10 space probe flew past Jupiter in 1973.

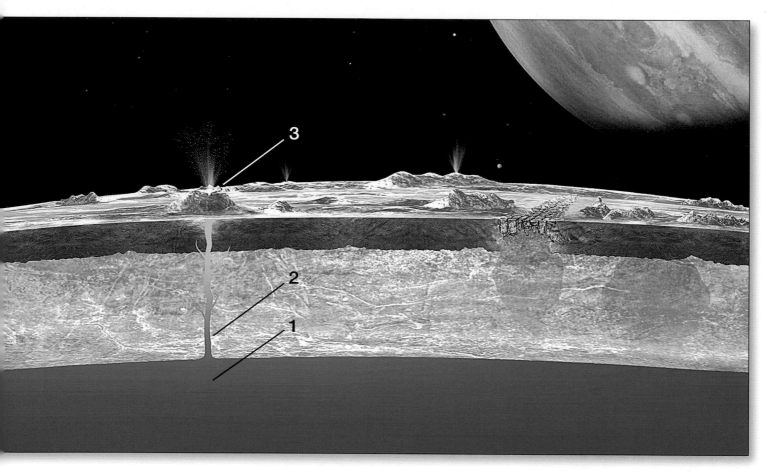

→ **Why should we study Jupiter?**

It's the biggest planet in the Solar System, and has at least 67 known moons. Several of these moons have icy surfaces. Scientists think vast oceans of water might exist underneath.

→ **Why is finding water so important?**

Living things need water. If icy moons have water, there might be some form of life. Icy moons are worth exploring.

↑ **This diagram shows what geologists think is under the frozen landscape of Jupiter's moon, Europa. Water (1) forces its way through cracks (2) in the thick ice layer, and explodes on the surface (3) as an "icecano."**

→ What is the JUICE mission?

JUICE is short for Jupiter Icy Moons Explorer. The European Space Agency (ESA) is due to launch this craft in 2022. It will map three moons—Callisto, Europa, and Ganymede—to see if they have hidden oceans of water. JUICE will provide information for future missions that will land on the moons.

↑ JUICE flies by a cutout view of Jupiter's moon, Ganymede. Scientists think the moon has a hot core that warms an ocean of water under the frozen outer layers.

IS A PROBE NEAR JUPITER NOW?

NASA's Juno probe (right) went into orbit around Jupiter in 2016. Its five-year survey program includes precisely measuring the strength of Jupiter's gravity and magnetic fields. Also, Juno may help to determine how the giant planet formed.

→ When could a lander visit a Jupiter icy moon?

Russian scientists have already designed a probe called Laplace-P, to land on Ganymede. It could perhaps fly with JUICE, or more likely, fly on a separate mission.

LIFE ON SATURN'S MOONS?

Enceladus and Titan are moons of Saturn. They were studied by the Cassini space probe, sent by NASA and European space agencies.

Huygens landed on the surface of Titan

➔ Where did the Cassini probe explore?

Cassini studied Saturn and its 62-plus moons from 2004-17. In 2005, Cassini released the Huygens probe, which landed on Titan, Saturn's largest moon. It found an incredibly cold environment, yet one with weather, rivers, and seas.

⬆ **A low pass over Enceladus in 2017 enabled Cassini to confirm that huge water fountains spray from an ocean under the icy surface.**

➔ What happened to Cassini?

Scientists plunged Cassini into Saturn's atmosphere so it would burn up on entry. This eliminated the risk the probe would contaminate a moon with Earthly organisms.

→ Are future missions to Saturn's moons being planned?

None are currently planned, but there are several advanced ideas, including a submarine (right) that could explore Titan's ultra-cold, liquid **methane** sea called Ligeia Mare. This sea is bigger than Lake Superior on Earth. It has a shoreline more than 1240 miles (2000 km) long.

→ A robotic submarine could explore Ligeia Mare, which is more than 550 feet (170 m) deep.

ALIENS IN HIDDEN OCEANS?

The likeliest homes for alien life in the Solar System are thought to be among the icy moons of Jupiter and Saturn—especially Europa and Enceladus.

Right now though, no one expects to find anything more advanced than a few simple cells.

→ Could Titan support life?

Ligeia Mare and other seas are on Titan's surface. They are far too cold for Earth-type life to survive. But some scientists wonder if a weird form of alien life might use methane there in the same way we use water. A submarine could check out that possibility. Titan might also have an ocean of water hidden deep below its chilly surface.

VOYAGE INTO DARKNESS

NASA's New Horizons probe flew past the dwarf planet Pluto in 2015. It is now in the Kuiper belt, far beyond the planets.

The Kuiper belt is a disc of mainly icy material beyond Neptune

→ Where is New Horizons going?

It is heading farther into the Kuiper belt. This disc-shaped zone contains material left over from when our Solar System first formed. There are three dwarf planets—Pluto, Haumea, and Makemake—and countless smaller objects.

↑ New Horizons is about the size of a grand piano. Here the probe is seen passing Charon, biggest moon of the dwarf planet, Pluto.

→ What are KBOs?

KBO stands for Kuiper Belt Object, and there are billions of them. Most are thought to be made of ice formed by frozen methane, ammonia, and water.

What is the next target for New Horizons?

This was discovered by researchers using the Hubble Space Telescope. They found a far distant KBO they called 2014 MU69. As planned, New Horizons should fly by MU69 in January, 2019. Measurements made with the HST reveal that MU69 is about 30 miles (48 km) across.

⬆ In 2019, the New Horizons probe will pass MU69. The KBO moves slowly through space, circling the Sun at no more than walking pace.

What will MU69 be made of?

MU69 is likely to be a large chunk of icy material, thought to be red in color. But we know little about MU69, so anything that New Horizons finds will be a fresh discovery.

HOW FAR AWAY IS MU69?

MU69 orbits the Sun at a huge distance, more than 43 times farther away than Earth's orbit. MU69 is so faint that it cannot be detected by telescopes on Earth. The HST (right) was used to search for this and other New Horizons targets.

PLANETS OF OTHER STARS

An exoplanet is a planet orbiting a star other than our Sun. The first exoplanet was discovered in 1992. Since then, thousands more have been found.

→ Where is the nearest exoplanet to us?

Proxima Centauri b is an exoplanet which orbits around the nearest star to the Solar System. Part of a star system called Alpha Centauri, Proxima Centauri b is about 1.3 times bigger than Earth. A "year" lasts just 11.2 Earth days threre. Radiation from its sun, Proxima Centauri, has probably blown away any atmosphere there, making it not **habitable**.

b   c   d   e   f   g   h

↑ TRAPPIST-1 and its family of exoplanets. When new planets are found, they are named after the star they orbit, followed by a letter. These are usually in alphabetical order, from nearest to farthest.

→ Could exoplanets support life?

We don't know of any for certain, but in 2017 a team found seven planets orbiting a small, cool star called TRAPPIST-1.

These planets are unusual because they are all Earth-sized rocky worlds. The three closest to their sun might even be habitable. The others are farther but may have water.

TRAPPIST-1 is only a little larger than the planet Jupiter, which is about as small as a star can be. Its heat is only half that of the Sun, but the exoplanets orbit it closely.

→ Where does the name TRAPPIST-1 come from?

The star is named after the telescope that discovered it. The Transiting Planets and Planetesimals Small Telescope is made up of two electronically-linked devices in Chile and Morocco. Run by the University of Liege in Belgium, and the Geneva Observatory in Switzerland, the astronomy team toasted the discovery with a Belgian drink called trappist beer.

↑ A possible view from the surface of a TRAPPIST-1 exoplanet. Apart from the dim star itself, two of the six other nearby planets move slowly across the alien sky.

→ Are other telescopes used to find exoplanets?

The Spitzer and Kepler space telescopes have a strong record. Spitzer helped to confirm the TRAPPIST-1 findings. By mid-2017, Kepler had recorded 2335 confirmed exoplanets.

WHY DO WE USE SPACE TELESCOPES?

The main reason is simple: to get them out of Earth's atmosphere. Delicate telescopic lenses operate much better if they don't have to cope with shifting air caused by heat, or pollution from towns and cities.

Kepler space telescope

STARSHOT TO ALPHA CENTAURI

 Project Starshot is a plan to build a fleet of tiny spacecraft, or nanocraft, fast enough to reach the nearest star system in 20 years or less.

A laser beam will push spacecraft at high speed

↑ Starshot will combine the power of hundreds of lasers into one high-energy beam. This will be aimed at tiny spacecraft, called Starchips. They could reach speeds of up to 37,000 miles/second (60,000 km/sec).

→ Who came up with the Starshot concept?
The team behind the idea of a light-powered nanocraft was led by the British physicist Stephen Hawking and Yuri Milner, a Russian science investor and physicist.

→ How will Starshot work?
Starshot will use the pressure of **laser** light to accelerate a fleet of very small spacecraft to an incredibly high speed.

→ How many Starchips?

By the 2030s, the Starshot fleet could consist of 1,000 or more tiny Starchips, each just 0.4 inches (10 mm) across. They will take about five years to reach the three stars of the **Alpha Centauri** system, which is about 4 light years from our Sun.

WHAT IS A LIGHT YEAR?

It's the unit used to measure the huge distances between stars. A light year is simply how far light travels in a year, traveling at about 186,000 miles/sec (300,000 km/sec). One light year is equal to some 5.9 trillion miles (9.5 trillion km).

↑ **A Starchip has an electronic core, surrounded by a square "sail" which uses light energy from lasers for forward motion.**

→ What is the target?

Micro-cameras aboard each Starchip will aim to take fly-by pictures of Proxima Centauri b, an exoplanet found in 2016. Proxima Centauri is a dim red sun, the smallest of three stars that make up the Alpha Centauri system. The picture here shows two designs of craft powered by light: a group of super-tiny, gold Starchips, and the slightly larger silver kite design. In a third concept, the Starchip is shaped like a tiny sphere.

SPACESHIPS OF THE FAR FUTURE

Will humans explore beyond our Solar System? New **propulsion** systems may one day allow us to travel as far as we wish.

Could warp drive from science fiction become a reality?

➜ Could we build a crewed starship?

The main problem is that the Universe is BIG. Using today's rocket technology, a trip to even the nearest star would take hundreds of years. Perhaps a human crew could be placed into a deep-sleep hibernation state, or deep-frozen, to be warmed and woken by robotic machines at journey's end.

⬆ Alcubierre's theories have also been worked on by a NASA team, headed by Harold Sonny White. The starship design here resulted from their detailed studies.

➜ Is there another answer?

The Mexican physicist Miguel Alcubierre has suggested a hyper-fast "warp drive" concept. A spaceship might travel much like the craft of the sci-fi TV show Star Trek.

➜ How would being able to warp space help?

According to Alcubierre's theories, it may be possible to warp space, that is, to shrink and expand space around a spaceship. The ship could then "surf" from star to star, by creating a zone of warped space around it. However, Alcubierre's idea is only a theory for now. It might be centuries before it becomes a reality.

➜ Future rovers might explore the desert moon of a distant exoplanet. This illustration imagines tall structures looming over the moonscape. Perhaps they are giant alien lifeforms, or maybe rocky formations, caused by eruptions from deep beneath the moon's surface.

WHERE TO EXPLORE NEXT?

Even without a warp drive, Starchips or similar craft may explore nearby stars and their exoplanets. And there is still plenty to explore in our Solar System.

In the near future, humans and robots will return to our Moon—this time to stay. The planet Mars beckons, too. In the late 2020s or early 2030s, we could land on the red planet, to explore and perhaps set up a colony for human settlement.

GLOSSARY

Alpha Centauri The nearest group of stars to our Solar System. Alpha Centauri consists of three close stars, Alpha, Beta and Proxima.

Apollo The US Moon landing program. Twelve Apollo astronauts landed on the Moon, during six Apollo missions, from 1969-72.

artificial satellite Spacecraft that orbits another space object, such as a planet or moon

asteroid Rocky bodies too small to be called planets that orbit the Sun

cells Tiny units that make up every living thing. Most plants and animals are made of millions of connected cells.

comet Icy bodies that releases gases as they orbit the Sun

habitable Having the qualities that make a planet able to support life, such as being the right distance from a star

infrared Situated outside the visible light spectrum at its red end

ISS The International Space Station, a base that orbits Earth at a height of about 250 miles (400 km), and holds a crew of up to six astronauts

laser Extremely concentrated beam of light, whose rays do not quickly spread out and lose their power

methane On Earth, a flammable gas used largely for heating. But on Saturn's moon Titan, methane exists as an ultra-cold liquid. There are methane lakes and seas on Titan, at about -292°F (-180°C).

NASA National Aeronautics and Space Administration, the US space agency formed in 1958

orbit A curving path through space by one object around a bigger one. Many orbits are nearly circular, such as Earth's path around the Sun. Others may be oval-shaped, such as the looping paths taken by comets.

pressure The weight of gas molecules pressing down on a planet

propulsion A means to create a forward-pushing motion

radiation A type of wave energy found in nature, such as visible light or infra-red heat radiation

robot, robotic A machine that can carry out complex instructions, with no human on hand to operate it

rover A space exploration vehicle designed to move across the surface of a planet

Solar System The Sun and planets, plus moons, comets, asteroids, and other space matter

Soyuz Russian crewed spacecraft, in service since 1967. The latest Soyuz MS has seats for three, and is used for flights to and from the ISS.

space telescope A telescope based in space, rather than on Earth.

↑ **The exoplanet Proxima Centauri b may look like this.**

About 20 were in service by 2017, examples being the Hubble, Kepler, MOST, and Spitzer. The James Webb space telescope will be used from the 2020s.

Trojan Asteroids that share a planet's orbit. The two biggest Trojan groups share the same orbit around the Sun as Jupiter.

wind turbine Propeller-like system that captures the energy in moving air, and converts it to electricity

People mentioned in the book:

Alcubierre, Miguel (1964-) Mexican physicist who came up with the concept of warping space as a way of making hyper-fast space travel possible

Aldrin, Buzz (1930-) The second human to set foot on the Moon. Aldrin was the Apollo 11 Lunar Module pilot.

Armstrong, Neil (1930-2012) The Mission Commander of Apollo 11, he was the first human to step on the Moon, on July 21, 1969

Gagarin, Yuri (1934-68) The first man to fly into orbit around Earth, on April 12, 1961

Hawking, Stephen (1942-) British physicist. Famed for his advanced theoretical science research, and an author of popular science books.

Landis, Geoffrey (1955-) US scientist working for NASA. He also writes award-winning sci-fi books.

Milner, Yuri (1961-) Russian investor and physicist, who launched Project Starshot in 2016, alongside Stephen Hawking and other experts

Webb, James (1906-92) NASA director in the 1960s. The new James Webb Space Telescope is named after him.

White, Harold Sonny (1965-) US NASA scientist, known for his work in developing Alcubierre's warp-drive theories

INDEX

airship 15
alien life 16, 17, 18, 21
ammonia 22
Apollo 2, 5, 7, 9, 11
artificial satellite 2, 4
asteroid 4, 7, 12, 13
   16 Psyche 13
   Trojans 12
atmosphere 17, 20

carbon dioxide 14, 15
comet 4

dwarf planets 4, 22
   Charon 22
   Haumea 22
   Makemake 22
   Pluto 4, 5, 22

exoplanet 24, 29

global warming 15
Google lunar X-Prize 8

hibernation 28

'icecano' 18
ISS 5, 7, 9

KBO, Kuiper belt 22
   MU69 23

laser 26
LEO 5
light year 27

methane 21, 22

Moon 2, 4, 5, 7, 8, 9, 29
   base 5
   flights 6
moons 4, 17, 18, 20, 21, 22
   Callisto 19
   Enceladus 20, 21
   Europa 18, 19, 21
   Ganymede 19
   Titan 20, 21

nanocraft 26
NASA 11, 17
orbit 4

people
   Alcubierre, Miguel 28, 29
   Aldrin, Buzz 2
   Armstrong, Neil 2
   Cernan, Eugen 8
   Gagarin, Yuri 2
   Hawking, Stephen 26
   Landis, Geoffrey 15
   Milner, Yuri 26
   Webb, James 11, 12
   White, Harold Sonny 28
places
   Geneva University
   Grand Canyon 16
   Lake Superior 21
   Liege, University of 25
   Ligeia Mare 21
   Olympus Mons 16
   Utah 12
   Valles Marineris 16
planet 4, 22, 24
   Earth 2, 4, 7, 12, 14, 15,
     16, 21, 23, 24, 25

Jupiter 4, 5, 12, 18, 19, 21,
   24
Mars 4, 5, 9, 13, 16, 29
Mercury 4
Neptune 4, 5, 22
Saturn 4, 20, 21
Uranus 4
Venus 4, 14, 15

robot 5

Solar System 4, 5, 12, 13, 15,
   18, 21, 22, 24, 28, 29
space collisions 13
spacecraft
   Boeing Starliner 7
   Dragon V2 6, 7, 9
   Orion 9
space launchers
   Ariane 5 11
   Blue Origin 6, 9
   Falcon (range) 6
   ITS 6
   New Glenn 6
   Saturn V 6
   SLS 6, 9
   Soyuz 6, 7
   Space Shuttle 6, 10
space probes 12, 18
   Bennu 12
   Cassini 20
   Chang'e 3 8
   Huygens 20
   Juno 19
   Lucy 12, 13
   New Horizons 5, 22, 23
   OSIRIS-REx 12, 13

Pioneer 10 18
Psyche 12, 13
Sputnik 1 2
Starshot, Starchip 26, 27,
   29
Venera 10 14
space telescope
   Hubble 10, 23
   JWST 10, 11
   JUICE 18
   Kepler 25
   Laplace-P 19
   MOST 11
   Spitzer 25
SpaceX 5, 6, 9, 17
stars 4, 24, 26
   Alpha Centauri 27
   Proxima Centauri b 24, 27
   TRAPPIST-1 24, 25
starship 28
sulfuric acid 15
Sun 4, 24

radar 17
rover 16, 17, 29
   Mars 2020 17
   Curiosity 16, 17
   Sojourner 16
   submarine 21
   Venus 14

warp drive 28, 29
water oceans 18, 19,

ABOUT THE AUTHOR

David Jefferis has written more than 100 non-fiction books on science, technology, and futures.

His works include a seminal series called World of the Future, as well as more than 30 other science books for Crabtree Publishing.

David's merits include the London Times Educational Supplement Award, and also Best Science Books of the Year.

Follow David online at: www.davidjefferis.com